Also by Judith Viorst

POEMS

The Village Square

It's Hard to Be Hip Over Thirty and Other Tragedies of Married Life

People and Other Aggravations

How Did I Get to Be Forty and Other Atrocities

If I Were in Charge of the World and Other Worries

When Did I Stop Being Twenty and Other Injustices

Forever Fifty and Other Negotiations

Sad Underwear and Other Complications

Suddenly Sixty and Other Shocks of Later Life

I'm Too Young to Be Seventy and Other Delusions

CHILDREN'S BOOKS

Sunday Morning

I'll Fix Anthony

Try It Again, Sam

The Tenth Good Thing About Barney

Alexander and the Terrible, Horrible, No Good, Very Bad Day

*My Mama Says There Aren't Any Zombies, Ghosts, Vampires,
Creatures, Demons, Monsters, Fiends, Goblins, or Things*

Rosie and Michael

Alexander, Who Used to Be Rich Last Sunday

The Good-bye Book

Earrings!

The Alphabet from Z to A (With Much Confusion on the Way)

*f*P

Unexpectedly Eighty

and Other Adaptations

Judith Viorst

Illustrated by Laura Gibson

FREE PRESS

New York   London   Toronto   Sydney

FREE PRESS
A Division of Simon & Schuster, Inc.
1230 Avenue of the Americas
New York, NY 10020

First Free Press hardcover edition October 2010

FREE PRESS and colophon are trademarks of Simon & Schuster, Inc.

For information about special discounts for bulk purchases,
please contact Simon & Schuster Special Sales at 1-866-506-1949
or business@simonandschuster.com.

The Simon & Schuster Speakers Bureau can bring authors to your live event.
For more information or to book an event contact the Simon & Schuster Speakers Bureau
at 1-866-248-3049 or visit our website at www.simonspeakers.com.

Manufactured in the United States of America

1   3   5   7   9   10   8   6   4   2

Library of Congress Cataloging-in-Publication Data
Viorst, Judith.
Unexpectedly eighty : and other adaptations / Judith Viorst ;
illustrated by Laura Gibson.
     p.   cm.
1. Aging—Poetry. I. Title.
PS3572.I6U54 2010
811'.54—dc22
2010004199

ISBN 978-1-4391-9029-6
ISBN 978-1-4391-9030-2 (ebook)

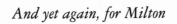

And yet again, for Milton

Lingering sunsets, stay a little longer.
—Gordon Jenkins

Contents

EIGHTYISH

EIGHTIER

EXCEEDINGLY EIGHTY

Unexpectedly Eighty

Eightyish

One Hallmark of Maturity
Is Having the Capacity to Hold Two
Opposing Ideas in Your Head at Once

My scalp is now showing.
My moles keep on growing.
My waistline and breasts have converged.
My teeth resist brightening.

I'm in decline.
It's positively frightening.

A new moon's arriving.
Sinatra is jiving.
My husband is holding my hand.
The white wine is chilling.

I'm still alive.
It's positively thrilling.

Driving at Night

December dinner parties do not thrive
Unless the dinner party ends at five.
Nor do we go to operas or ballets
Unless we're ticketed for matinees.
And when we take our grandkids on the town,
We must get back before the sun goes down.
Our social life is suffering from blight
As, one by one, we cease to drive at night.

We sensibly accept that we must squint
Whenever we confront the finer print.
We know our blusher cannot be applied
Unless our mirror's triple-magnified.
We count on bifocals to mend the blur
That sometimes makes a him look like a her.
But when the day is done, we're out of sight
As, one by one, we cease to drive at night.

Our new best friends may lack both charm and spark
But they can see the road when it is dark.
The widows bypass prepossessing guys
For schlumps possessed of twenty-twenty eyes.
And when it's evening and we're needing cars,
We'd pick up fellows (if we could) in bars.
We've grown to fear the fading of the light,
And, one by one, we cease to drive at night.

Been There, Done That

When I see a young woman strolling down the street
With her gleaming hair, glowing skin, and impeccable thighs,
Evoking from the passing male population
Some appreciative glances, some longing sighs,
Some politically incorrect but rave reviews,
And when I notice that none of these fellows is taking notice
          of me
In my elasticized-waistband pants and my comfortable shoes,
I mobilize the wisdom of a lifetime
And tell my envious heart, Been there, done that,
Calling upon my memory's rich store.
To which my envious heart replies,
Recalcitrantly, unreasonably,
But I want to be there again
And do that some more.

Up Here in Maine

So my husband and I are up here in Maine
With some of our children and grandchildren,
Vacationing together in an excessively rustic cabin in the woods,
The woods always having been a part of nature
I always have been happy not to commune with,
Although (on the grounds that at any age people can change),
I'm hoping to acquire a better attitude.

Everyone else is walking the trails, enjoying the
        pine-scented air and the crunch underfoot
And giving no thought to the fact that underfoot and in the air
        and everywhere else,
Danger is lurking.
And so, while I'm working hard on my better
        attitude
(On the grounds that at any age people can change),
I'm also thinking ticks and Lyme disease,
Whose "significant increase" in Maine, according to Google,
Is why I'm never walking through the woods
With my ankles exposed or my arms exposed or my head
        uncovered
Or minus my pepper spray,
Which I'm counting on to discourage the 22,000 foraging bears

Which, according to Google, have left their dens and are busily
        foraging
Across "eighty-five percent" of the state of Maine,
And whose record for killing human beings, though described as
        "remarkably low,"
Isn't really low enough to help me to acquire a better attitude,
Especially when these woods are home to the largest snake in
        Maine,
The black racer, aka *Coluber constrictor,*
Which, according to Google, needs protection from people like
        me
More than I need protection from snakes like it,
Even though it's six feet long, moves at "lightning speed,"
And is yet another reason why, thanks to Google
(And despite my belief that at any age people can change),
I've so far failed to acquire a better attitude.

What to Talk About

You'll find no even-tempered conversation
On matters like a misbehaving priest.
There's screaming over drug legalization.
There's snarling over peace in the Mideast.
Insist on global warming and there's tension.
Defend health-care reform and cast a pall.
On almost any subject you can mention
You'll stir up an unseemly free-for-all.

But there's one question that unites the pack:
Does anybody here have a bad back?

The world's your friend when speaking of the spine.
Civility is never put at risk.
So don't bring up intelligent design.
Stay focused on the herniated disc.
And though solutions vary:
Surgery or exercises?
A chiropractor or an orthopod?
There's animation rather than attack.

For everybody's sharing
And everybody's caring
When everybody talks of their bad back.

Ruth June

My mother
Wouldn't stop smoking
Until the lanky, red-haired doctor she adored
Told her, "Ruth—it's cigarettes or me,"
By which time she couldn't be rescued
From her implacable heart-disease genes,
Which accompanied her good-legs and excellent-cheekbones and
        killer-tournament-bridge-player genes,
None of which turned up in my DNA,
Though I did inherit her pleasure in books,

And her pleasure in women friends,
And her Persian lamb coat.

My mother
Was born in June and later, feeling a vacancy,
Chose her birth month for her middle name.
Married to marry, had kids because that's what was done.
Liked crossword puzzles, liked lilac trees,
Liked baking in the sun, and liked Bing Crosby.
She listened well, laughed wonderfully well, kept everybody's
      secrets.
Was probably better at being a friend than a wife.
And though I suspect that she probably wasn't wildly in love
      with her life,
In middle age she fell wildly in love:
With her grandchildren.

Ruth June,
I remember Lottie and Dottie and Tillie and Yetta and Pearl,
The women you called "the girls" and I called "aunts,"
Chattering on our screened-in porch,
In our breakfast nook,
In our sun parlor, over the phone.
All of them outlived you,
As I also—by two decades—have outlived you,
Though all of them were long gone before I finally figured out
The questions I wanted to ask them about
My mother.

Seeing Is Disbelieving

We just got the photos
Of our family vacation,
Three generations at play,
Looking happy and tan.
But who, I ask my husband,
Is that old lady?
And who, my husband asks me,
Is that old man?

Insurance, Eternity, John Quincy Adams, Polar Bears, Lab Tests, and So Forth

The clock in our bedroom says 2:17 in the morning.
I want to be sleeping, except I am thinking about
What I should serve at our dinner party next Friday.
Do we remain in the market, or get the hell out.
Whether the grandchildren know not to go with a stranger.
Whether I ought to consider replacing my knees.
If it is actually true that my lab tests are normal,
Or is nobody telling me I have a fatal disease.
And why I am thinking such thoughts at what the clock now
       says is 3:38 in the morning,

When I ought to be sleeping, except I can't sleep on my
       stomach,
And also can't sleep on my left side or right side or back
Because I am wondering if I have turned off the oven.
When to expect the next terrorist attack.
Whether we now have too much or too little insurance.
What can be done about my expanding behind.
Why other mothers get calls from their sons every Sunday.
Whether, if given the choice, to choose deaf over blind.

And how come I'm asking these questions at what my clock now
    says is 4:26 in the morning,

When I need to be sleeping, except I am prompted to ponder
The Briefness of Life. And Eternity. Also, The Void.
Whether my hair can get by one more week without color.
How to prevent polar bears from being destroyed.
I list all the presidents up to John Quincy Adams.
I add up the trips that I've made to the bathroom tonight.
I try to retrieve the name of my orthopedist,
The capital of Wyoming, the French word for "right."
I tally the losses sustained by my brain and my body,
Though none by either my weight or my appetite
Or by the number of things that still remain to be worried about
When the clock in our bedroom says time to get up in the
    morning.

House of Cards

*And every now and then, in the midst of some perfect
pleasure, maybe they will smile at their kids and say,
"You know, this reminds me of something I used to do with
my grandma."*

—Letty Cottin Pogrebin

Back when she was six, my youngest granddaughter and I
Would sit on the floor and build houses of cards together,
Ambitious and fragile constructions not long for this world,
This world I too am not too long for.

Will she remember our shared concentration?
Our heads, hers with wheat-colored curls, sometimes bumping
      each other?
Our knees, hers with cartooned Band-Aids, sometimes bumping
      each other?
Our hearts full of grandiose architectural plans?

Will she remember we steadied our fingers whenever we added
      a card,
Knowing the slightest of slips could bring the house down?
Will she remember we shallowed our breathing whenever we
      added a card,
Knowing that huffing and puffing could blow the house down?

Will she remember they kept falling down, and we kept picking
      up,
Restoring the rooms and expanding to two decks, then three,
Until our imperial dreams succumbed to carelessness or the
      giggles,
Until one of us—maybe her, maybe me—huffed and puffed?

Were we building something stronger than a house of cards?
Will she remember?

Fifty Years Later

Each morning we brush side by side in our double-sink
  bathroom,
And share Metamucil along with our multi-grain toast.
We search yet again through the house for our disappeared
  glasses
So we can read all the bad news in the *Times* and the *Post.*

He's 9:45 and I'm 10 at the dermatologist,
Which we'll follow by grocery shopping at Trader Joe's.
Tomorrow we'll sign up for classes in senior Pilates,
Then it's off to Assisted Living to see Cousin Rose.

Together we meet with our broker to get reassurance
That we'll die before there's no money to cover our bills.
Then we meet with our tax accountant to check on our broker.
Then we meet with our lawyer to write a few codicils.

He knows when he goes for his CAT scan that I'll gladly take
        him.
I know when I go for some blood work he'll come and he'll wait.
These are not like those torrid times on that beach in New
        Jersey,
But a date is a date.

 Eightier

How I Know I'm Old

I remember running boards, Victrolas, Frigidaires,
And when the really, really rich were merely millionaires,
And when it still was legal to start classes with school prayers.
    There was both good and bad in days of yore.
    But they don't write songs like "Stardust" anymore.

I remember double features and the Lindy Hop,
And sipping chocolate malteds at the local soda shop,
And when J. Edgar Hoover was our most admired cop.
    There were things both to cherish and deplore.
    But they don't write songs like "Stardust" anymore.

I remember *Our Gal Sunday* on the radio,
And watching television when the show was mostly snow,
And staying out of swimming pools because of polio.
    Yes, sometimes after's better than before.
    But they don't write songs like "Stardust" anymore.

I remember garter belts, long gloves, and the New Look,
And going all the way—I read about it in a book,
And when a homemade onion dip made you a gourmet cook.
    We've learned what to embrace and to ignore.
    But they don't write songs like "Stardust" anymore.

I remember back when hats were worn with business suits,
When women did the housework and their husbands the
    commutes,
When blackberries and apples were regarded just as fruits.
    But what, I'd like to ask, is progress for
    When they don't write songs like "Stardust" anymore?

Missing

Obladee, oblada, life goes on . . .
— The Beatles

I think I will miss myself more than anyone else will.
I miss myself now when I wake in the night, too aware,
With my eyes pinned wide-open,
My nails in my palms,
Breathing the darkest of air,
And imagine the world going on,
And on and on and on,
And on

And on
And on
And me not there.

I think I will miss myself more than anyone else will,
Myself as a part of this world that holds all I hold dear.
Since they make no exceptions
The time will arrive
When it's my turn to disappear,
And the world will keep going on,
And on
And on
And on.
How can the world still go on
If I'm not here?

Revelation?

When I awoke this morning
The world was radiant with newness.
Indoors and outdoors, all had been scrubbed clean.
The sky had achieved a blue that seemed beyond blueness.
Whites were whiter than white, greens greener than green.
And the edges of everything,
Windows
Walls
Tree trunks
Blades of grass,
Stood apart from the edges of everything else
With exquisite clarity.

How can I explain this? Revelation?
No—successful cataract operation.

Delia and Max

I looked for no marriage bond. I never sought anything in you but yourself.

—Heloise to Abelard

Let's hear it for Delia,
An older woman who snagged a younger man.
She's ninety; he's a lad of eighty-eight.
Though she isn't his Mrs. but merely his Ms.,
She's given her place up and moved into his.
And yes, she's contented to leave things as is,
So relax.
"I've got everything that I want," Delia says.
"I've got Max."

Let's hear it for Delia,
A wow of a widow whose friend of sixty years
Was widowered—so they began to date.

Now they're living together in what she calls sin,
Enjoying a life that seems strictly win-win,
While he's walking around with a permanent grin.
Is it sax?
"No comment," says Delia, then adds with a purr,
"I've got Max."

Let's hear it for Delia,
A lively lady teamed up with a lively gent.
Surely it's Kismet! It's Destiny! It's Fate!
If you're thinking their romance must soon lose its thrills
As they figure out which of them's paying what bills,
And reminding each other to take all their pills,
Here's some facts:
"None of that matters," says Delia.
"Just one thing matters," says Delia.
"And I've got what matters," says Delia.
"I've got Max."

Stopping by My Mirror
on a Sunny Morning

Whose breasts these are I think I know.
But have they always hung so low?
And when did my once perky rear
Begin to look like cookie dough?

Although I've crunched year after year
No stomach muscles yet appear,
Nor can I claim as a mistake
The size of thighs reflected here.

Reflection leads to pain and ache.
I wish that this damn mirror'd break
Or that I wouldn't care one peep
About the dents the decades make.

The price of vanity is steep.
But I've no time to whine and weep,
And pounds to lose before I sleep,
And pounds to lose before I sleep.

Among My Grandchildren

While I may point out, from time to time, that cheating at Pick
  Up Sticks
Deprives them of that inner satisfaction they can only achieve by
  playing fair and square,
And while, from time to time, I may deliver a little lecture
On not hurting people's feelings and changing their underpants,
And while I would never hesitate to prohibit the waterboarding
  of younger brothers,

Or discourage discussions of farting during meals,
I've decided that, for the most part, it is not my responsibility
To improve my grandchildrens' character
Or their hygiene.

Nor am I going to urge them to eat their vegetables.
Or tell them they need to look people straight in the eye.
Or remind them to pick up their toys and use a tissue not their
    sleeve and stop interrupting.
And though I hope they'll be taught
To be modest, responsible, generous, patient, and help set the
    table,
That isn't my job.

For I have chosen to be a three-desserts grandmother,
A yes-you-can-watch-another-video grandmother,
A why-don't-we-just-forget-your-bath-tonight grandmother,
A clap-and-cheer-and-shower-praise-on-them grandmother,
A grandmother who seditiously whispers in her grandchild's ear,
Don't tell your mom I let you do this—she'll kill me.
A grandmother who insists that it is the duty of the older
    generations
To improve and instruct the younger generations,
Except—except when I'm among my grandchildren.

Thinking About Great Sex

Entwined on the backseat of his old Ford,
Virginity respected—though deplored,
We 1950s girls knew how to play
Everything But . . . but never All The Way.

Then came the sixties, when they changed the rules
And self-restraint belonged to prudes and fools,
While women were instructed that we must
Enjoy full satisfaction of our lust.

No names like "slut" or "tramp" would be applied
To those who had their passions gratified,
Nor would folks ask, "What are you thinking of?"
If we were having sex, not making love.

Pursuing our desires just for fun
We freely finished what we had begun.
But, oh, that aching hunger, hot and sweet,
We still remember on his Ford's backseat.

Washington Dinner Party

(in Five Haikus)

1.
The Hostess Ponders Her Seating Arrangements

Pro-Life in between
Gay Marriage and Choice? Switch with
Two-State Solution.

2.
The Ambassador's Widow Observes She Is One of Nine Guests

Always the extra,
The add-on, the odd number.
My even is gone.

3.
The Senior Senator Vets His Dinner Partner

Wife of big donor.
Rapt listener. Nice cleavage.
I'll turn off my cell.

4.
The Out-of-Town Guest Is Confused

EO. SEC.
GSA. NLRB.
They're speaking in tongues.

5.
The Host Looks Around the Table and Has an Epiphany

The future belongs
To those who know pixels from
Bytes. That won't be us.

Easier

It's easier
To read in an empty room
And sleep all by yourself in a double bed
If you know that he's just out of town.

It's easier
To scramble a single egg
And sit up alone to watch the nightly news
If you know that he'll be coming home.

It's easier
To buy a ticket for one
And go solo to a movie or a play
If you know that he'll soon be around
To complain
Interrupt
Disagree
Leave his hair on the soap
Leave his dresser drawers open
Be picky
Be a pain in the ass
Be yours.

Exceedingly
Eighty

Exceedingly Eighty

> *Eighty is the new sixty.*
> —Ubiquitous

You still wear a size two with great flair,
And keep adding more blond to your hair,
Maybe started a late-life affair with a hot late-life guy.
But although you are nimble of brain and unflabby of thigh,
Eighty is not the new sixty.
Eighty is eighty.

All your panties are satin and lace.
And you move at a vigorous pace.
And you've had some work done on your face, which of course
    you'll deny.
If you must tell your age, you can tell a quite plausible lie.
But eighty is not the new sixty.
Eighty is eighty.

You get treatments to pep up your glands,
And erase those brown spots from your hands.
Whatsoever will slow down time's sands you are eager to try.

But the years that remain are in shorter and shorter supply.
And eighty is not the new sixty.
It's two decades older than sixty.
It's closer to ninety than sixty.
It's exactly halfway between one zero zero and sixty.
No, eighty is not the new sixty.
Eighty is eighty.

How to Stay Married

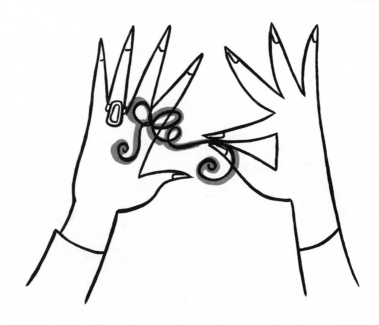

Whenever you try to recount all the
Hurts,
Disappointments,
Betrayals,
And grievances
That assail you,
May your memory fail you.

I Don't Intend to Gently Fade Away

I don't intend to gently fade away.
Though actuaries warn of coming night,
There's still a tune or two I'd like to play.

A ripened cheese and glass of Chardonnay
Continue to beguile my appetite.
I don't intend to gently fade away.

His hand on my bare shoulder can allay
The fear that passion's finally taken flight.
There's still a tune or two I'd like to play.

A grandchild's poem or masterpiece in clay
Has not yet ceased to fill me with delight.
I don't intend to gently fade away.

The world has much against which to inveigh,
But it remains beloved in my sight.
There's still a tune or two I'd like to play.

I hope to see another spring's array,
Another autumn's slanted golden light.
I don't intend to gently fade away.
There's still a tune or two I'd like to play.

An Afterlife

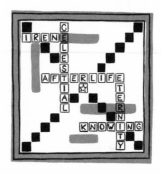

Although I don't believe in it,
My hopes for an Afterlife include
The everyday as well as the divine,
Which means that in addition to
Hanging out with heavenly hosts and hostesses,
Plus an assortment of other celestial beings,
I'd spend eternity with the people I love,
And never see those I could spend forever not seeing,
Particularly (please check attached list) my sister-in-law.

Although I'm not expecting it,
My plans for an Afterlife include
The frivolous as well as the profound,
Which means that in addition to
Grasping the ultimate nature of good and evil,
Plus how much of life is free will and how much is fate,
I'd be able to play the piano without taking lessons,

Eat whatever I want without gaining weight,
And get to have sex with Paul Newman without feeling guilty.

Although I wouldn't count on it,
My goals for an Afterlife include
The down-to-earth as well as the sublime,
Which means that in addition to
Purging my soul of sin and my heart of envy,
Plus ridding my spirit of selfishness and despair,
I'd concede that my friend Irene is better at Scrabble,
Admit that I haven't quite mastered learning to share,
And get over the fact that Fran Tepper, who—let me tell you—
       doesn't deserve this,
Is married to someone who worships the ground that she walks on.

Although I'm not disputing it,
My views of an Afterlife include
The dubious as well as the devout,
Which means that in addition to
My awe at the magnificence of creation,
I'm wondering what the creators were thinking about
When they decided, for instance, to make mosquitoes.
And weren't there any better options than death?
And why give a chronic skin disease to a darling person like
       Marilyn and a perfect complexion to a bitch like Beth?
And why leave us never knowing,
Never ever, for sure, really knowing
If there is an Afterlife?

Here at the Restaurant

Here at the restaurant,
After we three pairs of old, old friends
Have arranged ourselves to accommodate
A second back surgery, a recent bypass, a Parkinson's, and several
    hearing aids,
And after the one who can't see without her trifocals
Listens while her husband reads her the menu,
And after we have waved away the bread basket
And ordered our careful dinners of lean meat or fish with the
    sauce on the side, no potatoes just vegetables,
And before we start discussing
Personal trainer versus going to the gym.
Retirement home versus putting in an elevator.
And does anyone know a good gastroenterologist?
And is anyone else having trouble with their feet?
And should we be doing something with probiotics?
And can we really trust those generic drugs?
And is this normal forgetting or is it Al, Alz—what do they call
    that disease?
And just as we begin to clink our wineglasses,
Some of which hold sparkling water, not wine,
We smile at one another and make a toast that once seemed
    boring, but not anymore:

To health.
To health.
To health.
To health.
To health.
To health.

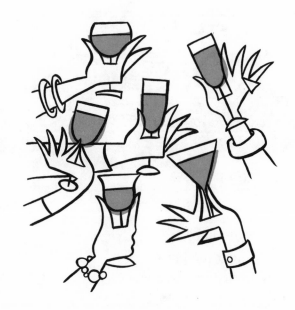

It's Not Too Late
to Give Up Being Cheap

To you who've spent a lifetime quite content
To leave a tip of under ten percent,
Whose pleasure in fine wines cannot be beat
But only if they're someone else's treat,
Who'll squeeze eleven pennies from a dime,
And reach to take the check—but not in time,
Although your parsimony may run deep,
It's not too late to give up being cheap.

To you whose soap comes only from hotels,
Who fishes quarters out of wishing wells,
Who'll cut the greenish parts away and eat
The far-too-long-expired deli meat,
Whose tube of toothpaste lasts and lasts and lasts,
Whose bargaining skills have never been surpassed,
While buying retail always makes you weep,
It's not too late to give up being cheap.

I know you surreptitiously regift,
I know that you can teach the thrift shops thrift,
And that you lie in bed on the same sheet
You bought the year of Adlai's first defeat.
But in this final segment, my old friend,
Forego tightfistedness and start to spend,
And though your assets sink, your heart will leap.
It's not too late to give up being cheap.

Just Because I'm Elderly Doesn't Mean You Can Talk to Me in Elderspeak

Don't call me honey.
Don't call me sweetie.
Don't call me darling or dear.
And don't shout in my ear.
I can hear what you're saying quite well.
I believe that your impudent query
Was, Who did you used to be, dearie?
To which I reply, sugarplum, lambie pie,
Go to hell.

E-Mail Is a Wonderful Way to Stay in Touch with the Children

They used to never write and never phone.
These days they also never e-mail back.
No matter how adorable my tone,
Each you've-got-mail is viewed as an attack.
My queries: "Do you hydrate?"
Observations: "Wool wears better."
And reminders: "Careless brushing leads to plaque."
Though all well meant, are viewed as an attack.

In order to provide them with a batch
Of articles I feel compelled to share,
I often, when I e-mail, click "attach."
But do they ever download? Not a prayer.
E. coli—where it's hiding.
Mortgage frauds—the latest victims.
And the theft of your identity—beware!
These must be read, but are they? Not a prayer.

My need to guide my children is intense,
But frankly they don't seem to give a damn.

Indeed, they've mobilized a strong defense—
They're sending all my e-mails straight to spam.
I'm trying to alert them
To the risks of daily living,
And to every epidemic, threat, and scam.
But I think they've turned their mother into spam.

After Giving the Matter
a Great Deal of Thought

After giving the matter a great deal of thought,
I've decided not to live longer than my husband.
Nor do I want him living longer than me,
Married to some younger woman who will want to redo my
      kitchen,
And bribe my grandchildren into being crazy about her,
And probably know a few sex tricks I've never heard of.

After giving the matter a great deal of thought,
I've decided life wouldn't be fun without my husband,
Nor would I want to start in with some other man,
With his whole new set of ailments,
And his whole new set of irritating habits,
And his difficult sons and daughters I would have to pretend
      to like,
No matter how definitively I didn't.

After giving the matter a great deal of thought,
I've decided my husband and I should die together,
Pleasantly and painlessly,

Of natural causes, of course,
And at a ripe old age, whatever that means,
Leaving behind our children to deal with the taxes,
The health insurance reimbursements,
That mess in the basement we planned to, but didn't, clear out,
And leaving them, too, to remember a marriage
Both wonderful and strenuous,
Actually, far more wonderful than strenuous,
Or so I have finally decided,
After giving the matter a great deal of thought.

Status Report

Too old to dream.
Too old to flirt.
Too old to sit and dish the dirt.
Too old to drink.
Too old to pet.
Too old to boogie.

Not quite yet.

About the Author

Judith Viorst was born and brought up in New Jersey, graduated from Rutgers University, moved to Greenwich Village, and has lived in Washington, D.C., since 1960, when she married Milton Viorst, a political writer. They have three sons—Anthony and Nick (who are lawyers) and Alexander (who finances affordable rental housing)—and seven grandchildren—Miranda, Brandeis, Olivia, Nathaniel, Benjamin, Isaac, and Toby. Viorst writes in many different areas: science books; children's picture books; adult fiction and nonfiction; poetry for children and adults; and three musicals, which are still performed on stages around the country.

About the Author

JUDITH VIORST was born and brought up in New Jersey, graduated from Rutgers University, moved to Greenwich Village, and has lived in Washington, D.C., since 1960, when she married Milton Viorst, a political writer. They have three sons—Anthony and Nick (who are lawyers) and Alexander (who finances affordable rental housing)—and seven grandchildren—Miranda, Brandeis, Olivia, Nathaniel, Benjamin, Isaac, and Toby. Viorst writes in many different areas: science books; children's picture books; adult fiction and nonfiction; poetry for children and adults; and three musicals, which are still performed on stages around the country.